Ben Can Run
and
Sam Is Fun

PHASE 2

/ss/

Level 1 – Pink

BookLife
Readers

Helpful Hints for Reading at Home

The graphemes (written letters) and phonemes (units of sound) used throughout this series are aligned with Letters and Sounds. This offers a consistent approach to learning whether reading at home or in the classroom.

HERE IS A LIST OF NEW PHONEMES FOR THIS PHASE OF LEARNING. AN EXAMPLE OF THE PRONUNCIATION CAN BE FOUND IN BRACKETS.

Phase 2			
s (sat)	a (cat)	t (tap)	p (tap)
i (pin)	n (net)	m (man)	d (dog)
g (go)	o (sock)	c (cat)	k (kin)
ck (sack)	e (elf)	u (up)	r (rabbit)
h (hut)	b (ball)	f (fish)	ff (off)
l (lip)	ll (ball)	ss (hiss)	

HERE ARE SOME WORDS WHICH YOUR CHILD MAY FIND TRICKY.

Phase 2 Tricky Words			
the	to	I	no
go	into		

TOP TIPS FOR HELPING YOUR CHILD TO READ:

- Allow children time to break down unfamiliar words into units of sound and then encourage children to string these sounds together to create the word.

- Encourage your child to point out any focus phonics when they are used.

- Read through the book more than once to grow confidence.

- Ask simple questions about the text to assess understanding.

- Encourage children to use illustrations as prompts.

PHASE 2

/ss/

This book focuses on the phoneme /ss/ and is a pink level 1 book band.

Ben Can Run
and
Sam Is Fun

Written by
Robin Twiddy &
Rod Barkman

Illustrated by
Drue Rintoul &
Paula Ramos

Can you say this sound and draw it with your finger?

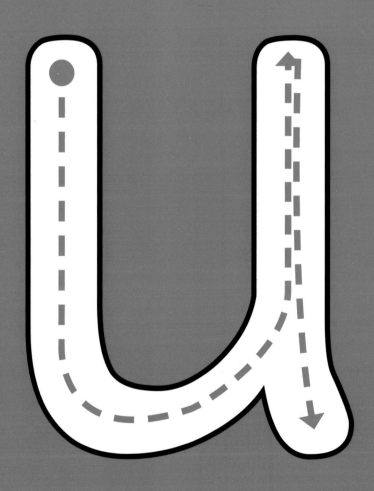

Ben Can Run

Written by
Robin Twiddy

Illustrated by
Drue Rintoul

Ben can run.

Ben can hop.

Ben hops in the mud.

HOP, HOP, HOP!

Ben is in a mess.

Ben is sad.

Mum gets the mud off.

Ben can run.

Ben can hop.

No, Ben, not in the mud!

Can you say this sound and draw it with your finger?

Sal, Sam, Pam and dog.

©2021 **BookLife Publishing Ltd.**
King's Lynn, Norfolk PE30 4LS

ISBN 978-1-83927-861-7

Ben Can Run
Written by Robin Twiddy
Illustrated by Drue Rintoul
Sam Is Fun
Written by Rod Barkman
Illustrated by Paula Ramos

An Introduction to BookLife Readers...

Our Readers have been specifically created in line with the London Institute of Education's approach to book banding and are phonetically decodable and ordered to support each phase of the Letters and Sounds document.

Each book has been created to provide the best possible reading and learning experience. Our aim is to share our love of books with children, providing both emerging readers and prolific page-turners with beautiful books that are guaranteed to provoke interest and learning, regardless of ability.

BOOK BAND GRADED using the Institute of Education's approach to levelling.

PHONETICALLY DECODABLE supporting each phase of Letters and Sounds.

EXERCISES AND QUESTIONS to offer reinforcement and to ascertain comprehension.

BEAUTIFULLY ILLUSTRATED to inspire and provoke engagement, providing a variety of styles for the reader to enjoy whilst reading through the series.

AUTHOR INSIGHT: **ROBIN TWIDDY**
Robin Twiddy possesses a Cambridge-based first class honours degree in psychosocial studies. He also holds a certificate in Teaching in the Lifelong Sector, and a post graduate certificate in Consumer Psychology. A father of two, Robin has written over 70 titles for BookLife.

AUTHOR INSIGHT: **ROD BARKMAN**
Rod Barkman is one of BookLife Publishing's most integral members. Known to other staff as Reliant Rod, he is always trying to bring his work to a new level. Rod has written multiple books for BookLife Publishing, of which he is extremely proud. Rod is a keen traveller, voracious reader and animal lover.

PHASE 2
/ss/

This book focuses on the phoneme /ss/ and is a pink level 1 book band.